CONTENTS

Words that look like this are explained in the glossary on page 24.

WELCOME to the World of PREDATORS

Different animals have different ways of getting food.

Predators are animals that get food by hunting and eating other animals.

We are about to find out all about predator reptiles.

Reptiles are scaly, <u>**cold-blooded**</u> animals. They usually have a backbone.

NIGHTMARISH Nile
CROCODILES

When Nile crocodiles are fully grown, they are apex predators. This means that they do not have any predators themselves.

Sharp teeth and powerful muscles make these crocodiles excellent hunters.

They can eat animals as large as wildebeests or zebras.

DREADFUL Central Bearded DRAGONS

Central bearded dragons are named after the spiky scales around their chins. They can puff these out to look scarier.

These predators hunt with their sticky tongues.

They quickly flick them out and pull insects back into their mouths.

AWFUL Green ANACONDAS

Some snakes kill their <u>prey</u> by wrapping themselves around them and squeezing tightly.

Green anacondas are one of these snakes.

Green anacondas can open their mouths wide to swallow prey whole.

A big meal may last them a few weeks.

TERRIBLE Alligator Snapping
TURTLES

Alligator snapping turtles are some of the largest turtles in the world.

These reptiles mostly live in the water.

This turtle has a worm-like <u>lure</u> on its tongue.

LURE

When animals come to see the lure, they get snapped up.

POWERFUL Reticulated PYTHONS

Reticulated pythons are the longest snakes in the world.

They are great at swimming and climbing trees.

These snakes can find prey even in darkness because they can <u>sense</u> heat.

When hunting, reticulated pythons squeeze their prey to death.

MEAN Gila
MONSTERS

One way that Gila monsters get food is by stealing eggs from other animals' nests.

They also hunt.

16

Gila monsters are 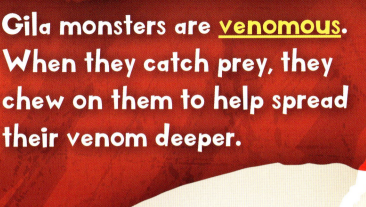**venomous**. When they catch prey, they chew on them to help spread their venom deeper.

KILLER King COBRAS

A king cobra's bite is venomous enough to kill an animal as large as an elephant.

When it is scared, this snake spreads out a hood on its head and hisses. This scares off other animals.

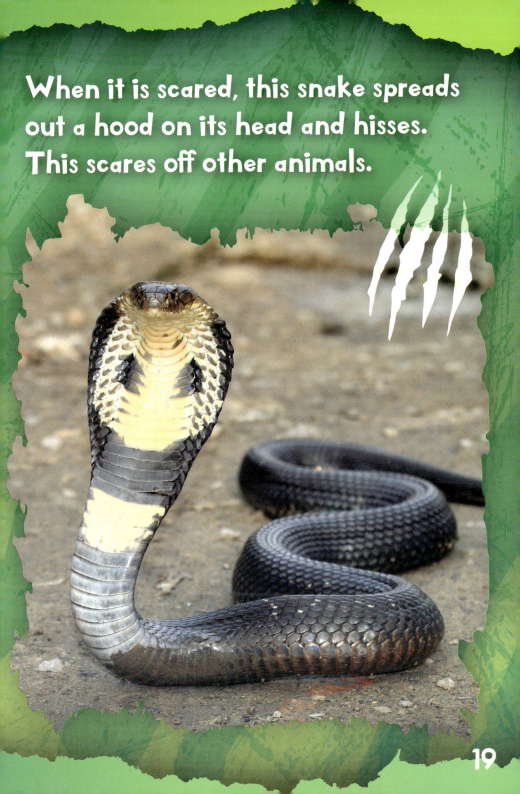

DEADLY Komodo
DRAGONS

Komodo dragons are the largest lizards in the world. They will eat whatever prey they can find.

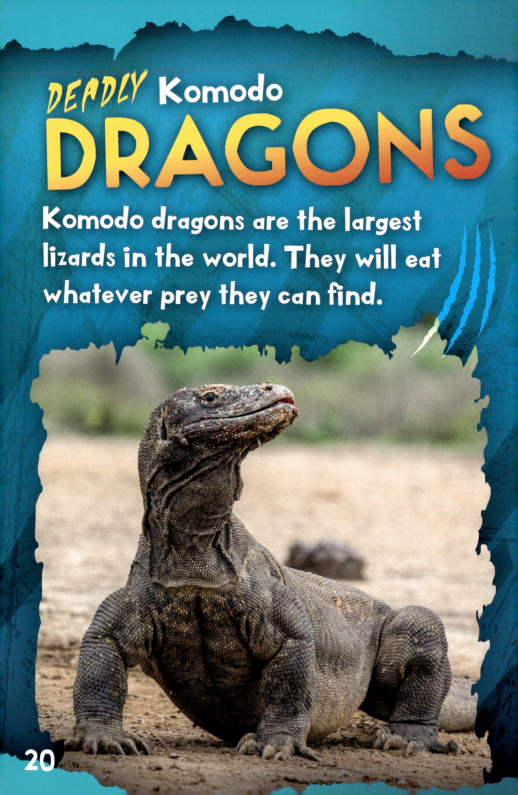

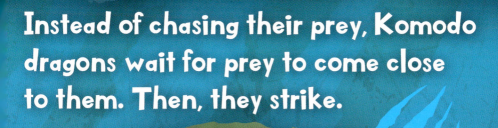

Instead of chasing their prey, Komodo dragons wait for prey to come close to them. Then, they strike.

RUTHLESS and RAVENOUS

Whether they are poisoning their prey or snapping up a snack, reptiles are dangerously powerful predators.

These ruthless reptiles come in all sorts of shapes and sizes.

Each one is terrifying in its own way!

GLOSSARY

COLD-BLOODED animals that have a body temperature that changes with the temperature around them

LURE something that attracts an animal to do something

PREY animals that are hunted by other animals for food

SENSE to feel or be aware of

VENOMOUS able to poison another animal or person through a bite or sting

INDEX